The ABCs of Proverbs

The Word to the Wise:
An Introduction to Proverbs

MARY K. TURKINGTON

WESTBOW
PRESS®
A DIVISION OF THOMAS NELSON
& ZONDERVAN

Scripture taken from the Holy Bible, NEW INTERNATIONAL VERSION®. Copyright © 1973, 1978, 1984, 2011 by Biblica, Inc. All rights reserved worldwide. Used by permission. NEW INTERNATIONAL VERSION® and NIV® are registered trademarks of Biblica, Inc. Use of either trademark for the offering of goods or services requires the prior written consent of Biblica US, Inc.

Scripture taken from the King James Version of the Bible.

WestBow Press books may be ordered through booksellers or by contacting:

WestBow Press
A Division of Thomas Nelson & Zondervan
1663 Liberty Drive
Bloomington, IN 47403
www.westbowpress.com
1 (866) 928-1240

ISBN: 978-1-5127-5521-3 (sc)
ISBN: 978-1-5127-5523-7 (hc)
ISBN: 978-1-5127-5522-0 (e)

Library of Congress Control Number: 2016914273

Print information available on the last page.

WestBow Press rev. date: 09/16/2016

This book is in memory of Mom and Dad, who
did their best to bring their wayward child up
in the nurture and admonition of the Lord.

Dear Reader,

Thank you for taking the time to read this little book. It has been prepared for you with much study and prayer. I hope you will be blessed by it.

The writings have been set up as devotional readings, so the goal is not for them to be read all at one time—or even one each day. Rather, as you look at each section, there are in some cases not only a key verse or verses but also other verses listed below the meditation and prayer for further consideration. Please take the time, perhaps even another day or two, to consider the key verses and any additional verses that may be added. Each one has something to say to you. Spiritual growth is not necessarily indicated by the amount of scripture you read but on the time you spend praying and meditating on each verse, asking God to open your heart to His message to you.

In these meditations, I have tried to be consistent with the truth of the Bible as proclaimed throughout His Word. However, I will be the first to admit that my words are only true insofar as they agree with and reiterate His. Therefore, I urge you to test what I say against the whole Word of God, that you may with confidence accept and abide by His teachings and count them your own.

If there are themes running through this offering, they are:

1. Jesus' words to "Love the Lord your God with all your heart and with all your soul and with all your mind and with all your strength ... Love your neighbor as yourself" (Mark 12:30, 31).
2. Study God's Word—the manual for living a blessed life. May this be the desire of your heart as you consider these readings and God's Word.

Take care, and God bless.

Mary

PS: When I nervously requested my friends C. B. Nagel and Keith McMahan to write the endorsements and Sue Nagel to write the foreword for this book, I emphasized that I was anxious to have them comment on the book only if they felt God was leading them to do so. I wanted them to know that if they felt at all uncomfortable in doing this, they shouldn't just do it for friendship's sake.

Upon receiving their responses, I was taken back by their comments about me and felt they should leave out that part, which they would not do (probably because they are such godly folks themselves, that is what they see in others). Please know that if the words in this book are helpful, the only One who deserves any praise is the good Lord Himself, for without His blessing and presence in my life, I am naturally a self-centered and prideful person. However, by knowing this, if you find the book a blessing in spite of my flaws, maybe it will encourage you in your faith walk to know that God can use you, too, even though you may feel you have things in your life that God needs to work on.

Thanks again to you for taking the time to consider my offering and to the Lord who has guided me in this endeavor.

Foreword

I have known Mary most of my life and can truly say she is a Proverbs 31 woman. She is a woman of great depth of character, kindness, wisdom, and love. As I read *The ABCs of Proverbs,* I feel as though I am sitting with Mary and listening to her words of wisdom as we enjoy a cup of coffee together. She continues to direct my heart and spirit to God's Word and *His wisdom*, love, grace, and goodness. She writes of praise to God for His faithfulness, about our sorrow for sin, and of the wonder of what Jesus Christ did for us.

This much-needed book gives us knowledge and appreciation of Solomon, whose wisdom from God forged and rescued his life. The same God offers us His wisdom still.

With this simple ABC format, we can think of what we need at the moment—help with fear, losing a pet, finding wisdom, walking in integrity—and go straight to the Proverbs to give us hope and guidance. Mary shows us how each proverb pertains to each of our lives. This format will also help us memorize these proverbs and keep God's Word safe in our hearts to draw upon forever. We worship the living God as we read His living words of wisdom.

Thy word is a lamp unto my feet

And a light unto my path.

—Psalm 119:105

Mary has written this book for the glory of God, in the spirit of Paul's encouragement to us. "Whatever you do, work at it with all your heart, as working for the Lord not for men." (Colossians 3:23) She also helps the reader hunger for more and more of His Word. *The ABCs of Proverbs* is inspirational and educational. These spiritual truths and the precious way Mary has shared them will change your life forever and inspire you to glorify God.

Day and night they never stop saying,

Holy, holy, holy is the Lord God Almighty,

Who was and is and is to come.

—Revelation 4:8b

Susan Myer Nagel

Cru (Campus Crusade for Christ International)

About the Book of Proverbs

Surely the words in Proverbs were not given simply to read and philosophize on but to take to heart and live out in our daily lives. The thoughts and wisdom given here are not simply Solomon's words or words of other wise men but the words of God that He inspired them to write.

Unfortunately, Solomon, who is credited with writing most of this book, ignored much of these words of wisdom himself as he got older. Instead of focusing on God and appreciating God's overwhelming bounteous goodness to him, as he became ever more rich and powerful, he took on wives and concubines in excess—even for those days and that culture—and worst of all, he chose them from people who served false gods. Their influence and his seemingly uncontrollable lust and pride in material goods drew his mind and heart from the very Source of all that he had been blessed with, and he built temples to those abominable gods.

God works through even our disobedience. This can be seen in other writings of Solomon as witnessed in Ecclesiastes where Solomon tells us of his disillusionment with everything "under the sun," describing it as vanity. He speaks of materialism, of trying "everything" but finding that nothing satisfies. As long as he pursues happiness—even wisdom—without God as the center of his life, he is frustrated and dissatisfied. He becomes so depressed that he, who had more in earthly treasures than any man on earth at the time, thought it would be better to be dead than alive. He even said never being born was preferable to being born and seeing all the evil done "under the sun." (See Ecclesiastes 4:2, 3.) However, at the close of his book of Ecclesiastes, he recognizes that man is called upon to fear God and keep His commandments.

Undoubtedly, his folly in straying from worshipping God and drowning himself in the illicit pleasures and worldly wealth brought him to recognize that with all his wisdom, he had become perhaps the greatest fool of all.

Unfortunately, the fruit of his ungodly ways was developed and harvested when his son, Rehoboam, succeeded him to his throne at his death. Because of Rehoboam's waywardness, he surrounded himself with young men who obviously had no thought of seeking God's wisdom. They advised him foolishly in reigning over his kingdom, and because of his callousness toward his subjects, Rehoboam brought on a rebellion by his people. The kingdom was forever split—with David's line retaining only two tribes and the others deserting to Jeroboam, whom they made their king.

What a different outcome Israel might have had if Solomon had practiced what he preached. Telling someone, "Don't do as I do, but do as I say," seldom influences those to whom the advice is given. Living a prayerful, godly life will be far more effective in causing others to take your words seriously than any amount of teaching or preaching not matched by actions.

As we contemplate the selected verses on the following pages, may our prayer be that the dear Lord will help us to not only read and speak His Word but to also live it faithfully.

Authors

Although the majority of Proverbs is authored by Solomon, there are some that are attributed to others. The following is the breakdown according to author:

- the proverbs of Solomon, son of David, king of Israel (Proverbs 1:1–22:16)
- Pay attention and listen to the sayings of the wise; apply your heart to what I teach. (Proverbs 22:17–24:35)[1]
- more proverbs of Solomon, copied by the men of Hezekiah, king of Judah (Proverbs 25:1–29:27)
- the sayings of Agur, son of Jakeh—an oracle (This man declared to Ithiel to Ithiel and to Ucal.) (Proverbs 30:1–33)
- the sayings of King Lemuel: an oracle his mother taught him (Proverbs 31:1–31)

PLEASE NOTE: All scriptures are taken from the New International Version unless otherwise indicated. KJV equals King James Version

A is for **Animal**

A righteous man cares for the needs of his <u>animal</u>,
but the kindest acts of the wicked are cruel.
—Proverbs 12:10

Perhaps you have heard people say, "A dog is man's best friend," or maybe you've said it yourself. Others feel that way about their horse. We speak of our pets—cats, birds, whatever—as being like one of the family. And the good Lord knows that many of these creatures are very loyal and loving toward us. Some are so smart they can be trained to not only do tricks but also lead the blind, sniff out illegal drugs, guard their masters, detect imminent seizures, and more. When something happens to them, we feel the pain of their loss and, more often than not, shed tears.

There's nothing in the Bible that speaks plainly about seeing our beloved pets again after death; however, when the new heaven and earth is established, the scriptures say in Isaiah 11:6–8,

> The wolf will live with the lamb, the leopard will lie down with the goat, the calf and the lion and the yearling together; and a little child will lead them. The cow will feed with the bear, their young will lie down together, and the lion will eat straw like the ox.

The infant will play near the hole of the cobra, and
the young child put his hand into the viper's nest.

So if all these animals will be a part of the kingdom, it's possible that we will see our dear pets again.

However, in spite of these scriptures, there's no indication that animals have souls. When man was created, he was the only creature created in the image of God, and he was given dominion over all the animals. So as much as we love our pets, they were not made in the image of God. Though He wants us to be kind to animals, He does not want us to give them priority over man. Yet in our upside-down, topsy-turvy world where evil is good and good is evil, we find some animal rights' activists who are also proponents of killing babies in the womb.

What's wrong with this picture? When we give greater importance to animals than we do to man, our thinking has become grievously skewed, and God is not pleased. The two greatest commandments Jesus told us are "Love the Lord your God with all your heart and with all your soul and with all your mind and with all your strength" and "Love your neighbor as yourself" (Mark 12:30, 31). Jesus also said that if we love Him, we are to keep His commandments. (See John 14:15.)

While we have been given dominion over all other creatures (Psalm 8:6–8), that does not mean that we have the right to make them suffer needlessly. To kill for sport and not for the purpose of protecting ourselves or to provide food for our table is surely not pleasing to Him. Therefore, let us look at God's creation through His eyes as much as possible and keep our priorities straight in dealing with our fellow man and the other creatures He has made.

Prayer: Dear God, thank You for the gift of life so freely given to us and to our beloved pets. Help us to treasure every human being—in the womb or elderly, healthy or afflicted, and yes, those who have committed atrocities, praying for their salvation even as we punish them for their crimes.

Sometimes, Lord, it is so tempting for us to elevate our dear pets above other humans, especially if those humans are guilty of hateful acts. At times like that, instill in us a genuine concern for the life that has gone astray, and help us to have the wisdom to deal with them according to Your will.

We are so grateful for our pets and all the varieties of birds and animals and creatures in the waters that You have so generously provided for our good and our pleasure. What a blessing they are to us, and what joy our pets bring us. May we never forget You, the source of all our blessings.

In Jesus' name we offer our praise and thanks to You. Amen.

 is for **Bury**

The sluggard <u>buries</u> his hand in the dish; he
will not even bring it back to his mouth!
—Proverbs 19:24

The sluggard <u>buries</u> his hand in the dish; he
is too lazy to bring it back to his mouth.
—Proverbs 26:15

When a verse is repeated twice, as in the verses above, it seems it
must have some special significance. Why would verses that speak
about a sluggard's laziness be important to reiterate? Could there be
a meaning beyond the obvious?

Perhaps there is another lesson here for us to consider. Our first
thought might be that we are certainly not lazy people. We have a job
which we are very conscientious about; we take care of our property;
we volunteer our time to different organizations. So it appears we can
ignore these proverbs or perhaps use them as fodder against others
who appear to us to be lazy.

However, it may be that the subject of laziness is not only about
our physical habits. Could it be that we are lazy in our spiritual
life? Do we bury ourselves under the covers of our beds on Sunday
mornings on a regular basis? Do we choose watching television or
using the Internet over attending a Bible study? Do we immerse

ourselves in our work rather than taking time daily to read God's Word and pray? Do we religiously allot time to our physical health while neglecting to spend even minutes on our spiritual health?

We obviously must work to support ourselves and take care of the things God has allowed us to have; however, do we take the time to thank Him for the abilities He has given us to do these things. We couldn't work if we were not given at birth the capacity to develop our minds and our bodies; yet often we take these things for granted.

If we consider ourselves Christians, loving the Lord should be our first priority. However, we often are too lazy to read His Word. We can find time (hours at a time often) to invest in almost any alternative activity. Making the effort to spend time with Him, however, seems too much for us—though praying, picking up our Bible and reading it is more a matter of discipline than effort.

Most of us have at least one Bible or New Testament in our home. We don't have to "order it in" or "fix it" as we do a meal. We really don't have to do anything beyond asking God to help us understand what we are reading. So are we spiritual sluggards too lazy to even pick up the spiritual food that God has provided for us?

A young man's father recently died unexpectedly. The young man was devastated. He considered his dad his best friend. Every evening he would call or text his dad, and they often met with friends and played their guitars together. In fact, they had a little band in which they performed. It was done out of sheer love and the joy they had in one another. This is the kind of relationship God wants with us.

Are you a spiritual sluggard? Have you laid a Bible next to your bed or on the bookshelf but are too lazy to pick it up? How is your relationship with your heavenly Father? Have you become spiritually lazy and neglected the One Who is the Source of physical, mental, emotional, and spiritual health? Now's a good time to start counting your blessings and show your love to the One Who loved you so much that He gave His life for you. Make a pact now with your

Father to spend time each day visiting with Him. He will bless you for it.

Prayer: Abba,[1] Father, please help us not to be so spiritually lazy that we neglect to spend time with You each day—a special time of prayer and reading Your Word. However, help us also to be aware of Your presence all day long, sending up little pleases and thank-yous as we go about our daily tasks, that we may honor and bless You in everything we do. In Jesus' name we pray. Amen.

---

[1] Abba is a word used by Jesus for God. It is a very personal expression in the Aramaic language for "Father," similar to how a child would say, "Daddy," to his beloved father.

 is for **Counsel**

Perfume and incense bring joy to the heart, and the pleasantness of one's friend springs from his earnest <u>counsel</u>.
—Proverbs 27:9

For most of us, the soft, gentle aroma of a delicate perfume relaxes us and gives us a sense of well-being. Even so, when we have a friend who will seriously but gently give us good advice, we feel very blessed. If we have someone with whom we can openly share our thoughts and feelings and in turn be given an honest response, we are rich beyond measure.

There are some acquaintances whom we would never want to open our hearts to, for we know that any advice or comment they would make would be harsh and judgmental. On the other hand, there are some who would agree with us on everything, whose ideas always coincide with ours, never pointing out those things which could eventually lead us into serious difficulties.

The perfect friend is one who, though not judgmental of us, nevertheless provides counsel which may, at times, be contrary to decisions we would make, giving us the opportunity to re-think our choices and consider ideas which had not occurred to us before. Such a friend is a gift, a rare treasure.

Of course, no earthly friend is perfect and all wise; however, if we choose to accept Him, God Himself will be our greatest friend. We remember the words of an old hymn:

What a Friend we have in Jesus, All our sins and griefs to bear;
What a privilege to carry Ev'rything to God in prayer.
Oh, what peace we often forfeit! Oh, what needless pain we bear,
All because we do not carry Ev'rything to God in prayer.

Have we trials and temptations? Is there trouble anywhere?
We should never be discouraged, Take it to the Lord in prayer.
Can we find a Friend so faithful, who will all our sorrows share?
Jesus knows our ev'ry weakness; Take it to the Lord in prayer.

Are we weak and heavy laden, Cumbered with a load of care?
Precious Savior, still our refuge,- Take it to the Lord in prayer.
Do thy friends despise, forsake thee? Take it to the Lord in prayer;
In His arms He'll take and shield thee; Thou wilt find a solace there.[2]

As we take our concerns—temptations and all—to Jesus, He will direct through His Word and give us the counsel we need. At other times, He will give us wisdom to choose earthly friends who will encourage and help us in our decision making.

No matter what our problems, worries, or concerns are, Jesus will provide us with the answer if we are willing to seek His wisdom and wait on His answer—whether through His Word, through a godly friend, or through our conscience—as we mature in our relationship with Him.

Prayer: Gentle Jesus, dearest Friend, be our closest companion and guide. Provide us with Your wisdom as we face our daily responsibilities and the temptations and problems that go with them. Help us to remember to look to You and be willing to follow You as we seek Your counsel. Give us godly friends who love us enough to speak up when they see us making unwise decisions. Thank You, dear Savior. Amen.

(Additional emphases on having good counsel are shown in the proverbs below.)

> Counsel and sound judgment are mine; I [wisdom]
> have understanding and power. By me kings reign
> and rulers make laws that are just; by me princes
> govern and all nobles who rule on earth.
> —Proverbs 8:14–16

> Plans fail for lack of counsel, but with
> many advisers they succeed.
> —Proverbs 15:22

> Have I not written thirty sayings for you, sayings of counsel
> and knowledge, teaching you true and reliable words, so
> that you can give sound answers to him who sent you?
> —Proverbs 22:20, 21

 is for **Defend**

Speak up for those who cannot speak for themselves,
for the rights of all who are destitute. Speak up and
judge fairly; <u>defend</u> the rights of the poor and needy.
—Proverbs 31:8, 9

Our first reaction to this verse would probably be to wholeheartedly agree with this sentiment. Of course we should stand up for the underdog. We live in a country where people, no matter what their status in the economic scale, should be guaranteed fair treatment.

Yet how easy it is to ignore the daily slaughter of preborn babies—all in the name of a woman's "want to." We give such murder high-sounding names like "a woman's right to choose" or a way to preserve a woman's "quality of life."

Proverbs 24:11, 12 says,

> Rescue those being led away to death; hold back those staggering toward slaughter. If you say, "But we knew nothing about this," does not He who weighs the heart perceive it? Does not He who guards your life know it? Will He not repay each person according to what he has done?

There was a time when, because of our ignorance and lack of technical knowledge, we could think and say that this growth inside of us was not human yet, and to reinforce that thought and ease our conscience, it was easy to call this growth a "fetus," which sounded less human than "baby."

Now that our technology has increased, it has become plain that this growth is not just a blob of tissue but a baby, and not only is it recognizable as such very early on in its development, but it is also capable of feeling pain. There's not a day goes by but hundreds of babies face death by various procedures, such as poisoning in the womb or partial-birth abortion—both extremely painful to the child. We can no longer claim innocence when the subject of abortion is discussed and say, "But we knew nothing about this."

This devotional is not written to stigmatize those who have had abortions, for God loves each one of us as well as our babies and is so ready to forgive us of sin, whatever it may be, if we confess and repent of them. We all can confidently know that our relationship with Him is secure when we do this. Which one of us is sinless?

We are not all called to participate in a protest in front of an abortion clinic, but we are all called to speak up when injustice is done. This may take the form of supporting those who have a public presence and declaiming such procedures by volunteering our time and/or our finances toward a pro-life agency that assists those who are afraid or unable to care for the child in their womb—or at the least, when the subject comes up, speak lovingly but firmly against the baby killing. Perhaps the greatest deterrent of all to this procedure is faithfulness in prayer for all those associated with the crime—whether the baby victims, the mothers (many times barely more than children themselves, and some honestly believing they are doing the right thing), the pro-life support groups and organizations, couples longing to adopt, and yes, even those who are performing the procedures in this genocide, that they may be given the eyes to see and the heart to feel compassion for the victims of this billion-dollar industry.

Prayer: Holy, merciful, compassionate Father, put in our hearts a love for everyone in any way involved in this destruction of innocent children, whether it is those who are in the business of performing the dreadful acts, those who feel they are facing an impossible situation, or those who are striving to protect the babies and preserve their lives. May we never excuse ourselves from the responsibility of doing whatever You lead us to do in taking up the cause of these precious little ones. In the name of Jesus, Who welcomed the children with open arms, we pray. Amen.

 is for **Enemy**

If your <u>enemy</u> is hungry, give him food to
eat; if he is thirsty, give him water to drink.
In doing this, you will heap burning coals on
his head, and the LORD will reward you.
—Proverbs 25:21, 22

At first glance, these verses seem to indicate that if you treat your
enemy with kind deeds, it will bring disaster upon him and the Lord
will bless you for it. In other words, the purpose of being kind to
your enemy is not only so that you will be rewarded by the Lord but
also so that you will, in a sense, get revenge on him, for who would
want burning coals heaped upon their head?

Interestingly, in Romans 12:19, 20, Paul repeats these verses in
this setting.

> Do not take revenge, my friends, but leave room for
> God's wrath, for it is written: "It is mine to avenge; I
> will repay," says the Lord. On the contrary: "If your
> enemy is hungry, feed him; if he is thirsty, give him
> something to drink. In doing this, you will heap
> burning coals on his head." Do not be overcome by
> evil, but overcome evil with good.

Although this scripture indicates that our enemies will be judged by the Lord and He will mete out punishment on them if we are kind to them, should that be the reason for our kindness to them? First John 3:15 tells us that our very thoughts, as well as our actions, can condemn us. "Anyone who hates his brother is a murderer, and you know that no murderer has eternal life in him." So when we are kind to our enemies for the purpose of "getting back" at him, are we really loving our neighbor as ourselves?

Somewhere an article was printed (and it may have been in a newsletter from Wycliffe Bible Translators) that at the time when these key verses were penned, there were, of course, no stoves or furnaces as such; the way you heated your home or your oven was with hot coals. If those coals somehow burned out, a person would have to go to his neighbor and request that he be given some burning coals to take back to his home. Whether it was water from the river or coals from a neighbor's oven, they would be carried in a container on a person's head. When we understand these verses in this setting, it gives a whole new aspect to the scripture and we can see that "heaping coals of fire on his head" would be a real blessing to our enemy, which would be done out of kindness—not revenge. And who knows? Just maybe such kindness would result in our adversary coming to know our beloved Lord himself.

Prayer: Loving and forgiving Lord, make us loving and forgiving also, so that when we are mistreated by others, we will not only forgive them but kindly and prayerfully provide for their needs if called to do so. Amen.

(See verses below to give us further enlightenment about what the consideration of "enemy" might entail.)

> When a man's ways are pleasing to the LORD, He
> makes even his <u>enemies </u>live at peace with him.
> —Proverbs 16:7

Do not gloat when your <u>enemy</u> falls; when he stumbles,
do not let your heart rejoice or the LORD will see and
disapprove and turn His wrath away from him.
—Proverbs 24:17, 18

Wounds from a friend can be trusted,
but an <u>enemy</u> multiplies kisses.
—Proverbs 27:6

 is for **Find**

> Blessed is the man who <u>finds</u> wisdom, the man
> who gains understanding, for she is more profitable
> than silver and yields better returns than gold.
> —Proverbs 3:13, 14

It appears from this verse and the others below that wisdom is not something that comes naturally. Rather, it is something we must look for and actively seek. As we read through the Bible, words such as *understanding, knowledge, prudence, learning, discernment,* and *insight* are used pretty much as synonyms for *wisdom.* However, in today's world, there can be quite a difference in the meaning of *wisdom* and other synonyms such as *knowledge.*

World famous surgeon, Dr. Benjamin Carson said,

> I would emphasize, however, another favorite point: that wisdom is different from, and often more critical than, knowledge. Many use the terms wisdom and knowledge interchangeably. They are, however, quite different, and having one in no way confers the other. Knowledge is familiarity with facts. The more knowledge one has, the more things one is capable of doing, but only with wisdom is one able to discern

which of the many things they are capable of doing should be pursued and in what order. [3]

Therefore, in considering how to find wisdom in today's terms, we would not necessarily be thinking of a college education or some other type of higher education as a source of learning true wisdom.

What then is the source of real wisdom, and how can we pursue it?

Since God is the Creator of all things, He is the Source of wisdom as well as knowledge, learning, and the other synonyms used on a regular basis in His Word. He *IS* wisdom, and as such can give us this attribute to discern how to use the knowledge He can and does provide when we search for wisdom.

Where do we search? We can learn much from studying His creation, by recognizing that there's no way this universe and all within it could come into place without an Intelligence so far beyond our imagination that we cannot even begin to grasp the complexities of Him. This can be the starting point of wisdom for those who have no access to the written Word. However, to begin to gain a relationship with this Intelligence, we must be able to go beyond the obvious signs of creation to the books written by those He inspired through the centuries and which have been incorporated into the one book we know today as the Bible.

There is no other book in the world which is so well documented—no other book which has been so determinedly destroyed through the ages and yet survived—as the Bible. Though this book and the God it reveals have been blasphemed, mocked, scorned, disrespected, insulted, banned, and in the case of God's Son, crucified, the book and its Author continue on, bringing life and love to those who are seeking the truth.

Simply reading God's Word, however, is not the key to wisdom. It must be searched and mined to its depths, and a commitment on the part of the reader must be made to the Author. We must recognize our own sinfulness as we plumb the depths of the love and mercy of the Source of all wisdom.

Let us, therefore, in our search for wisdom, go to His Word and kneel at the feet of Him Who gave His life for us, asking that He enter our lives as Lord and Savior. As He reveals Himself through His Word, He will also give us the key to wisdom that will give us the understanding of how to use the knowledge and learning we acquire through other sources. As it says in Matthew 6:33, "But seek first His kingdom and His righteousness, and all these things will be given to you as well."

Prayer: Our Father, we humbly bow before You as we recognize our own ignorance and Your wisdom, the depths of which we can never fathom. We ask that You give us a portion of this wisdom that we may lead lives that will be a blessing to others and will bring honor and glory to You. Thank You for Your Word that we may learn Your wisdom as You reveal it to us. In Jesus' dear name we pray. Amen.

(Jesus said, "Seek and ye shall find" [Matthew 7:7]. In the proverbs below, which are but a small sampling from many, we see how important it is to seek the right thing. If we seek wisdom, that is what we will find; however, if we seek other things, the results can be disastrous.)

> Then they will call to me, but I will not answer; they
> will look for me but will not <u>find</u> me. Since they hated
> knowledge and did not choose to fear the LORD … they
> will eat the fruit of their ways and be filled with the fruit
> of their schemes. For the waywardness of the simple will
> kill them, and the complacency of fools will destroy them.
> —Proverbs 1:28, 29 … 31, 32

> My son, if you accept my words and store
> up my commands within you, turning your

ear to wisdom and applying your heart to
understanding ... then you will understand the fear
of the LORD and <u>find</u> the knowledge of God.
—Proverbs 2:1, 2 ... 5

My son, pay attention to what I [wisdom] say; listen
closely to my words. Do not let them out of your sight,
keep them within your heart; for they are life to those
who <u>find</u> them and health to a man's whole body.
—Proverbs 4:20–22

I [wisdom] love those who love me, and those who
seek me <u>find</u> me. With me are riches and honor,
enduring wealth and prosperity. My fruit is better
than fine gold; what I yield surpasses choice silver.
—Proverbs 8:17–19

Now then, my sons, listen to me [wisdom]; blessed are
those who keep my ways ... For whoever <u>finds</u> me <u>finds</u>
life and receives favor from the LORD. But whoever fails
to <u>find</u> me harms himself; all who hate me love death.
—Proverbs 8:32 ... 35, 36

A fool <u>finds</u> pleasure in evil conduct, but a man
of understanding delights in wisdom.
—Proverbs 10:23

He who seeks good <u>finds</u> goodwill, but evil
comes to him who searches for it.
—Proverbs 11:27

He who pursues righteousness and love <u>finds</u> life,
prosperity and honor.
—Proverbs 21:21

 is for **Gossip**

The words of a <u>gossip</u> are like choice morsels;
they go down to a man's inmost parts.
—Proverbs 18:8

A <u>gossip</u> betrays a confidence; so avoid
a man who talks too much.
—Proverbs 20:19

The words of a <u>gossip</u> are like choice morsels;
they go down to a man's inmost parts.
—Proverbs 26:22

Here we have three verses—two of which are identical. Unfortunately, the words of 18:8 and 26:22 are so true. For some reason, we find great pleasure in hearing and sharing gossip—unless we are the object of it. In verse 20:19, we are warned against those who make this a habit.

It's interesting that these verses speak of men's involvement in gossip. Of course, men, in this case, refers to mankind. It seems in this day and time, however, we think more of women as being gossipers. Yet when the "good ol' boys" meet at their favorite coffee joint, how often the stories fly—and frequently without much discernment between truth and fiction.

"So what?" you might ask. Everyone does it. It's not like you're hurting anybody.

God has a very different opinion of those who betray a confidence, of those who keep the fire of dissension burning. In fact, in Romans 1:28–32, Paul points out to his readers that this sin (yes, sin) is just as evil as *murder* and that those who participate in this activity deserve to die.

Whoa! How harsh is that! Why would God so vehemently oppose such a "normal" activity?

If you wish to see gossip at its worse, consider the "scandal sheets" (commonly referred to as newspapers and magazines) which report the supposed activities of famous people, often ruining reputations and bringing heartache and shame—sometimes to the innocent. In fact, some of the victims have committed suicide because of the assassination of their character. And don't say that if it's true it's not gossip. Often whatever is being reported is not a proven fact, and if it is, then it should be handled in the courts (if it is a legal matter) before it is publicized. If it is not a legal matter, the concern should be to help the person get back on the right track, rather than making them fodder for gossip.

If we participate in spreading rumors, we are guilty before God of breaking the two greatest commandments: to love God and to love our neighbors as ourselves (Mark 12:30, 31).

So the next time you are visiting with others, guard your tongue and your ears. Don't stick around to listen to others' gossip, and don't repeat things you hear if you cannot avoid hearing them. As with other sins, this will take a lot of self-discipline, which really comes only by "praying continually" as commanded in 1 Thessalonians 5:17. That attitude of prayer will carry you through temptations as you allow the Holy Spirit to control your life.

Prayer: Dear God of perfection, You know we are unable to lead a blameless life, yet we long to be more like You. Help us to give the grace to others that You give to us, and if there is some way we can help another who has fallen, give us the heart to do so—not broadcasting their faults but helping to support and encourage them as they strive to change their ways. As sinners saved by grace, we pray this to You, our forgiving and loving Lord. Amen.

(Below are a few more verses to consider on this matter.)

A gossip betrays a confidence, but a
trustworthy man keeps a secret.
—Proverbs 11:13

A perverse man stirs up dissension, and
a gossip separates close friends.
—Proverbs 16:28

Without wood a fire goes out; without
gossip a quarrel dies down.
—Proverbs 26:20

is for **Hardens**

Blessed is the man who always fears the Lord, but
he who <u>hardens</u> his heart falls into trouble.
—Proverbs 28:14

Have you ever watched a two-year old determined to have his
own way? "No!" he shouts loudly, and often more than once, when
we try to correct him or her. That precious little one that so thrilled
us at birth and whom we love beyond life itself has seemingly
become an uncontrollable little monster. With many prayers and
determined discipline, eventually we are usually able to reign him
in, but the frustration and despair we sometimes feel along the way
can be overwhelming—especially when the child is our first and
we have had little experience in dealing with temper tantrums and
waywardness.

We suddenly realize that we are the parents of what we would
have termed "a spoiled brat" if we saw such behavior in other people's
children. We also realize how much we need the help of our heavenly
Father in dealing with the situation.

God loves us even more than we love our children, enough to
send His Son to die for us. Yet we blithely go our own way, ignoring
His commands and consequently often bringing upon ourselves
heartaches and pain. Just as our little children suffer sooner or later
when they disobey, so we are apt to find ourselves facing difficulties

of our own making when we are determined to do what we want regardless of the consequences.

Do you suppose our experience disciplining our little ones reflects the longing for obedience God feels toward us as we go about our daily activities, often giving little thought to His plan for our lives?

Could it be that whether consciously thinking so or not, we do not really want to spend too much time with God in His Word? Perhaps we might find that He wants to teach us what is best for us—and we already have made up our minds that we can take care of ourselves, thank you. Of course, when we or our loved ones get into serious difficulty, we don't have a problem telling God what we want Him to do to get us out, but as far as being willing to change our ways and bending to His will, we often have a hands-off attitude toward Him. We may not physically scream, "No!" as our little ones do, but essentially that is our attitude.

Proverbs 1:7 says, "The fear of the LORD is the beginning of knowledge, but fools despise wisdom and discipline." To turn our backs on God and think we can ignore our Creator is not only foolish but dangerous to our spiritual welfare. If we make this a habit, we will find ourselves getting into evil ways and becoming a part of the politically correct world we live in, where often black is portrayed as white and white, black.

Therefore, let us heed His Word and take it seriously, recognizing that if we insist on doing our own thing, God will allow us to suffer for it. He is an awesome God, and should we continuously refuse to acknowledge His authority and reject His Son, He will ultimately allow us to get our wish and be separated from Him for eternity.

Turn now to Him. Acknowledge His power and might, as well as His gift of love, and acquiesce to Him in repentance and obedience. Have the attitude of a little child who knows his daddy loves him but at the same time has a fear/respect for him—not because his father is a tyrant but because he knows that in disobedience he will be disciplined in order to save him from grief later on and to help him become all that he can be.

Prayer: Our Father in heaven, help us never to forget that You are holy, that You are creator of all things, that You are an awesome God. Impress on our minds Your absolute justice and our utter sinfulness so that we may appreciate Your immeasurable love in sacrificing Your Son for us. We give ourselves to You that we may be accepted into Your kingdom, knowing that only through Jesus may we come and be freed from an eternity separated from You. Thank You, thank You, thank You. Amen.

I is for **Integrity**

The man of <u>integrity</u> walks securely, but he who
takes crooked paths will be found out.
—Proverbs 10:9

What a blessing it is to be associated with a person of integrity. If he or she is your friend, you know you can trust the secrets of your heart to them. If he is your employer, you know he will be fair in his dealing with you. If she is an employee, you know you can depend on her honesty with you and your customers. Whatever the relationship might be, you can feel secure that there is no evil intent, that there will be no gossip or backstabbing from them.

On the other hand, how unpleasant and potentially harmful it is to be associated with someone who is dishonest, a liar, a gossip. Sometimes it takes a while to recognize them for what they are, especially if you yourself are honest, for it is easy to assume that others will be the same. How disappointing and sometimes disastrous it is to discover that someone in whom you put your trust has betrayed that trust.

We are warned in this verse that if we stray from a life of integrity, it will become apparent, so though we can seldom control someone else's conduct, we can control our own with God's help. If we walk daily with the Lord, reading His Word and praying, we will find ourselves being more like Him. When we do err, He will prick our conscience and we will not be comfortable in His presence until we confess our sin and make it right. Thankfully, He is always ready to forgive us, and being right with Him brings peace and an inner joy, even when things go wrong around us.

As we strive to live a life of integrity, let's seek out others who do the same that we may find strength, encouraging one another to do the right thing.

Prayer: Our Father, may our greatest desire be to serve You with integrity that Your goodness may be reflected in our lives—not to bring honor to ourselves but to cause others to see how great You are. Forgive us when we fail, and lift us up when we get discouraged at our weakness. Thank You for being the Source of all goodness and leading us in Your way. Amen.

(Integrity is the standard of the righteous and separates them from the unrighteous.)

The integrity of the upright guides them, but the
unfaithful are destroyed by their duplicity.
—Proverbs 11:3

Righteousness guards the man of integrity,
but wickedness overthrows the sinner.
—Proverbs 13:5

It is not good to punish an innocent man,
or to flog officials for their integrity.
—Proverbs 17:26

Bloodthirsty men hate a man of integrity
and seek to kill the upright.
—Proverbs 29:10

 is for **Joy**

A cheerful look brings <u>joy</u> to the heart, and
good news gives health to the bones.
—Proverbs 15:30

There are a lot of things that happen in our lives and in this world today that cause us to be disheartened, and it's easy for us to become discouraged. What a pleasure it is to meet someone who has a smile on their face and a cheerful word.

One way to avoid feeling depressed and gloomy is to read God's Word. In fact, *gospel* means "good news," and the four gospels—Matthew, Mark, Luke, and John—bring the ultimate good news. Of course, there's more to the Bible than the four gospels; the good news is spread throughout the Book of Books.

There are sixty-six books incorporated into the Bible and each one is history—*His story* of how much God loves us. From the first words of Genesis to the last words of Revelation, we learn of God's redemptive work with man. The Bible does not gloss over the sins of men, even godly men, but the way of salvation is shown to be always available to those who seek it.

In our world, there are a lot of health problems originally caused by sin and the loss of a perfect world. Many of our maladies are mental and emotional. Very often these problems are a result of our broken relationship with God. If we lack faith and trust in our Lord, we suffer all kinds of distress from worries, unforgiveness toward others, dissatisfaction with what we have, envy, jealousy, anger, and even hate. It is said that people with a positive attitude are healthier and recover more quickly from disease and accidents than those who are negative in their thoughts.

If we develop a relationship with our loving heavenly Father and seek His Holy Spirit to indwell us through acceptance of Christ as our Savior, He will change our thought patterns and we will truly be "born again"—not only in our spiritual life but also emotionally, mentally, and often even our physical being will respond positively.

Prayer: Dear Father, the Author of joy, impart to us Your delight and pleasure in the many blessings we have but frequently overlook. May we especially find joy and peace in the knowledge of Your love and care for us. In Jesus' dear name we pray. Amen.

(Joy is a fruit of the Spirit and the reward of those who love the Lord, for their actions are frequently the source of joy in others as well as themselves as evidenced in many of the verses below.)

A wise son brings joy to his father, but a
foolish son grief to his mother.
—Proverbs 10:1

The prospect of the righteous is joy, but the
hopes of the wicked come to nothing.
—Proverbs 10:28

When the righteous prosper, the city rejoices; when
the wicked perish, there are shouts of joy.
—Proverbs 11:10

There is deceit in the hearts of those who plot
evil, but <u>joy</u> for those who promote peace.
—Proverbs 12:20

A man finds <u>joy</u> in giving an apt reply—
and how good is a timely word!
—Proverbs 15:23

To have a fool for a son brings grief; there
is no <u>joy</u> for the father of a fool.
—Proverbs 17:21

When justice is done, it brings <u>joy</u> to the
righteous but terror to evildoers.
—Proverbs 21:15

is for **Kind**

He who is <u>kind</u> to the poor lends to the LORD,
and He will reward him for what he has done.
—Proverbs 19:17

It's so easy these days when times are tough and the economy is bad to think of ourselves as being poor. If we live in a country where we are not ruled by a despot but generally have the right to do or say pretty much what we please, we probably enjoy the opportunity to work and make some kind of living—though that is not always true.

There are among us those who, through no fault of their own, are destitute—sleeping in cars, tents, subway tunnels, even boxes on the street—and the problem seems to be getting worse. Periodically, particularly around Christmas, we are apt to hear and see news reports about them, and their needs are brought to our attention.

When we do learn of these dear folk, the emphasis is generally on their physical needs, and that problem certainly needs to be addressed, but most of the time they, and many who are in much better condition materially than they, are experiencing even greater poverty. That is the poverty of the Spirit. They are often without hope and the comfort that only the Holy Spirit can give them.

There are Christian organizations such as the Salvation Army that are seeking to meet more than just the physical needs of people. Their goal is to share the love of Jesus Christ—many times first in deed and then in word. If a person is starving and/or homeless, you will seldom be able to get their attention just by talking to them. They need to see love in a tangible form, such as food and housing. Then they can hear about the love of God through the actions of love displayed by His servants.

Jesus told his disciples in Mark 9:41 that we are to give to others in His name. Unfortunately, we have the temptation to give to others not only with the desire to help them but also perhaps because it makes us look good. We have no thought of bringing glory to the One who gave us what we are giving to others. Giving to others who are in need will undoubtedly be received with appreciation by those who receive it, and may make a real difference in their well-being for the moment. But giving in Jesus' name will often cause us (the givers) to make this more than a one-time instance. We will look beyond the obvious and give not only a material gift but also our time and effort in making a real difference in their lives, going on to invite them to have a relationship with Jesus Christ, the greatest gift of all.

As we look around us, let us be sensitive to those we come in contact with and be willing to share the ultimate gift—Christ's love—not cramming our faith down their throat but gently and lovingly as the Spirit leads, offering them the opportunity to know Him Who is the Source of all physical, mental, and spiritual goodness.

There's a story (source unknown) about a woman who was always thanking God for everything. Her neighbor was an atheist and hated hearing her always praising the Lord for His goodness.

One day he decided he'd show her that God was not the source of all good things, so he bought several bags of groceries and left them on her doorstep. The next day when he saw her, she began telling him how good God had been to her, providing her with several bags of groceries.

At this the man laughed and said, "I was the one who left the groceries on your steps, not God. So you see, God is not the source of all good things."

The woman also laughed and said, "Praise God. How wonderful of Him to provide the groceries—and even have you pay for them."

God does work in mysterious ways, and He can provide for our needs and those of others, often in ways that are completely unexpected. May we be God's hands and feet as we provide as best we can for those less fortunate than ourselves.

Prayer: Generous and holy Father, give us grateful hearts for providing so freely to us, and open our eyes to the needs of those around us so that we may, in turn, share our bounty with others. As we seek to help to meet others' physical needs, may we also have the heart to share from the abundance of our spiritual blessings, letting them know that we are simply the channels of Your love and goodness. In Jesus' name we pray, Amen.

(Often acts of kindness given from the heart bring blessings not only to the recipient but also to the donor, whereas the opposite is true for those who act unkindly as evidenced in the verses below.)

A <u>kindhearted</u> woman gains respect, but ruthless
men gain only wealth. A <u>kind</u> man benefits himself,
but a cruel man brings trouble on himself.
—Proverbs 11:16, 17

A righteous man cares for the needs of his animal,
but the <u>kindest</u> acts of the wicked are cruel.
—Proverbs 12:10

An anxious heart weighs a man down,
but a <u>kind</u> word cheers him up.
—Proverbs 12:25

He who despises his neighbor sins, but
blessed is he who is <u>kind</u> to the needy.
—Proverbs 14:21

He who oppresses the poor shows contempt for their
Maker, but whoever is <u>kind</u> to the needy honors God.
—Proverbs 14:31

He who increases his wealth by exorbitant interest
amasses it for another, who will be <u>kind</u> to the poor.
—Proverbs 28:8

 is for **Light**

The <u>light</u> of the righteous shines brightly, but
the lamp of the wicked is snuffed out.
—Proverbs 13:9

In the book of Acts, we read of a Pharisee by the name of Saul who was intent on persecuting and killing the followers of Jesus (Who by that time had died on the cross, been buried, risen again, and ascended to heaven). Jesus' disciples had been proclaiming Him as the Son of God, their Messiah, and Saul was sure this was heresy. He loved God; therefore, he believed that anyone who claimed that someone else could be God deserved to die. Saul was going to do his best to destroy them in order to preserve the holy name and sovereignty of the one and only God.

As he was traveling along the road to Damascus on his mission to purge the world of those who defiled God's name, the scriptures say,

> Suddenly a light from heaven flashed around him. He fell to the ground and heard a voice say to him, "Saul, Saul, why do you persecute me?" "Who are you, Lord?" Saul asked. "I am Jesus, Whom you are persecuting." He replied, "Now get up and go into the city, and you will be told what you must do."
>
> —Acts 9:3b–6

It appears that Saul's love for God had been genuine but misdirected. He didn't argue with His vision of Jesus but instead immediately knew this Jesus to be the Lord God. He allowed those traveling with him to lead him into Damascus (for he had been blinded by the light), where he fasted for three days.

In the meantime, God had spoken to a man named Ananias and told him to go to Saul and lay hands on him, blessing him and praying that God would fill him with the Holy Spirit. Although Ananias was reluctant to do so because he knew Saul's reputation of persecuting Christ followers, he obeyed God's instructions and did as he was told. In doing so, Saul's sight was restored and he began his life as an apostle of Jesus Christ.

Saul was the instrument God chose to use to spread the good news to the Gentiles. Eventually he traveled on four missionary journeys and is now recognized as Paul, the author of many books of the New Testament which he had originally written as letters to Christians in churches, many of which he established among the Gentiles. Those of us who are not of Jewish heritage might call him our spiritual ancestor.

Few of us will have an experience even close to that of Paul's. However, if we accept Christ as our Savior and love Him with all our being, we will walk in the path of righteousness as our Lord leads us. In the beginning, our light may not shine too brightly, for most of us have many things in our lives which need to be corrected as God convicts us of them. But as we continue our life in Him, He will shine through us more brightly each day. Our goal will become less and less centered around ourselves and more and more centered around ways we can serve God and bless those about us.

In this world, we may never be recognized as great, but when we are called to be with the Lord, we will receive the crown of life and we will indeed be brilliant as we reflect His light and love perfectly. What a fantastic day that will be!

Prayer: Light of the World, shine on us. Impart to us Your love and faithfulness so that we may reflect on this world in some small way the light of Your mercy and grace to others. In Jesus' name we ask this. Amen.

(In the additional verses below, we see that our light grows brighter as we walk in the ways of God.)

> The path of the righteous is like the first gleam of
> dawn, shining ever brighter till the full <u>light</u> of day.
> —Proverbs 4:18

> For [your father's commands] are a lamp, this teaching is a
> <u>light</u>, and the corrections of discipline are the way to life.
> —Proverbs 6:23

 is for **Mercy**

He who conceals his sins does not prosper, but
whoever confesses and renounces them finds <u>mercy</u>.
—Proverbs 28:13

If we confess our sins, He is faithful and just and will
forgive us our sins and purify us from all unrighteousness.
—John 1:9

These two verses, one from the Old Testament and one from the New Testament, help us to see God's mercy toward us. It seems on paper such an easy thing to do—to find mercy by confessing our sins. Yet it goes against our grain to do so. Which of us likes to admit we have sinned? It means humbling ourselves and acknowledging our frailties.

Often when we see our children being stubborn and refusing to admit they have done something wrong (even when they know it's apparent to us), we are irritated and forced to punish the child. We want them to confess so they can get right with us—show that they are sorry and want to do what is right in the future.

Why are they so obstinate? Why can't they just admit they're wrong? We really don't want to punish them for lying as well as for their other sin. In fact, if they seemed truly repentant, we would perhaps not have to punish them at all. Nevertheless, they insist on lying and trying to cover up their faults.

It's so easy to see others' sins, but do we see our own? Don't you suppose God feels the same way about us? Sometimes we can hide our sins from others, but we can never hide them from God. When we sin, it sets up a barrier between our loving Father and ourselves. Just as we grieve over our children being wayward, so He grieves over us. Many times we do have consequences to pay, just as our children do, in order that we may learn to obey. When we don't obey, we must confess and seek His forgiveness.

Because God is so merciful, when we do humble ourselves before Him and repent, He is faithful and just to forgive us, even making us pure in His eyes. Unlike ourselves, He is not one to store in His memory all our misdeeds if we have received forgiveness for them. In Psalm 103:12 we are told, "As far as the east is from the west, so far has He removed our transgressions from us." What a great promise that is.

God's faithfulness is shown in keeping His promise of forgiveness when we confess our sins. His justness is shown by having our sin, which is so abominable to Him, charged to the account of His Son Who took our place on the cross to cover the sins of all who will accept salvation through Him.

As our relationship with Him deepens, His will becomes more apparent and we will be eager to seek His forgiveness when we stray from His ways. May we show the same mercy to others whom we feel have betrayed our friendship.

Prayer: "Our Father, Which art in heaven, hallowed be Thy name. Thy kingdom come. Thy will be done, in earth, as it is in heaven. Give us this day our daily bread. And forgive us our debts, as we forgive our debtors. And lead us not into temptation, but deliver us from evil: For Thine is the kingdom, and the power, and the glory, forever."[2] Amen.

(When we exclude God from our lives, we exclude mercy toward others as evidenced below.

A poor man pleads for <u>mercy</u>, but a
rich man answers harshly.
—Proverbs 18:23

The wicked man craves evil; his neighbor
gets no <u>mercy</u> from him.
—Proverbs 21:10

[2] Matthew 6:9b–13 (KJV).

 is for **Now**

Do not say to your neighbor, "Come back later; I'll
give it tomorrow"—when you <u>now</u> have it with you.
—Proverbs 3:28

Many years ago, a church newsletter contained an article with
a picture of "A Round Tuit." The picture was pretty much just a
circle with the word "TUIT" imposed on it. The article encouraged
everyone to cut the circle out so they would have it available. There
seemed to be a problem with people delaying the completion of
activities with which they had indicated they would help, or maybe
procrastinating about doing those things they thought were good.
However, because they had other things that were more pleasant,
more effortless, or maybe just more fun, they couldn't get "a round
tuit." The little circle would hopefully remove their excuses.

Solomon advises us in this verse not to delay helping your
neighbor when you can just as easily satisfy his needs then.

We've heard the modern equivalent of this proverb. "Don't put
off till tomorrow what you can do today." Needless to say, we can't
do everything we're called upon to do, but there are some things that
should take priority in our lives. One of them is to take time each
day to read God's Word and pray. When we do this, then the good
Lord Himself helps us to prioritize other things in our lives. He gives
us the wisdom to know the important from the unimportant and

helps us to see how we can organize our time to the best advantage, always remembering God first and others second.

There are times when we need His wisdom to determine the "best" from the "okay" or even "good." We think of the story of the Good Samaritan and how the priest and the Levite passed by the injured man, probably so they could participate in or attend services, which in themselves are normally good choices. Leaving someone to die on the road, however, made those "good" choices bad. Hopefully, we will seek God's will each day and be led to serve God and serve others—getting "a round tuit" *NOW* rather than later.

Prayer: Heavenly Father, thank You for always hearing our prayers and doing those things for us which are for the best in Your perfect timing. Give us the wisdom to know what You would have us do now and the impetus to do it that perhaps we may be the answer to our neighbor's prayer. In Jesus' dear name we ask this. Amen.

(As can be seen in verse 7:11 below, we can choose to do evil now. Let each of our nows instead be chosen to do God's will.)

> Now then, my sons, listen to me; do
> not turn aside from what I say.
> —Proverbs 5:7

> [A woman dressed like a prostitute] is loud and
> defiant, her feet never stay at home; now in the street,
> now in the squares, at every corner she lurks.
> —Proverbs 7:11

<u>Now</u> then, my sons, listen to me; pay attention
to what I say. Do not let your heart turn to [the
adulteress'] ways or stray into her paths.
—Proverbs 7:24, 25

<u>Now</u> then, my sons, listen to me [wisdom];
blessed are those who keep my ways.
—Proverbs 8:32

is for **Opinions**

A fool finds no pleasure in understanding
but delights in airing his own <u>opinions</u>.
—Proverbs 18:2

Is there anything more annoying that being around someone who "knows it all" and is not afraid to enlighten you with it. Any kind of discussion or comment seems to cause this fellow to take over and declare "the truth" about the matter. It's impossible, it seems, to make a comment. Or if you make one, this know-it-all will argue the point, even if he has never had the experience or expertise to have authority in the matter.

People who persist in this attitude make plain their ignorance and are avoided like the plague. When others are forced into being in their presence, even when the know-it-all says something plausible, his words are suspect.

It is easy to recognize this kind of person—unless it is ourselves. Why is it we see other people's flaws so easily yet have a way of overlooking our own?

One way to ensure that we don't make a habit of becoming overzealous in our desire to share our esteemed opinions with others is to make a daily habit of going before the Lord in prayer and seeking His wisdom. We can glean real wisdom by prayerfully studying His Word and being open to what He has to say, not just spending the bulk of our time asking for things (although He wants us to confide all our cares and worries in Him, too).

Encompassed in this one book, the Bible, which is actually a library of sixty-six books, is so much wisdom that those who study it all their life still find new understandings and knowledge regularly as the Holy Spirit opens their eyes to them. A well-known pastor who has been preaching for more than fifty years one day said, off the cuff as he was preaching from the Word, "I never thought about this before until just now …" He went on to tell of a new thought he had about that scripture, though he had preached on it many times before.

So how about you? Are you interested in learning God's wisdom or in taking over a conversation, impressing (or trying to impress) everyone with your ideas? Step back and take a look at yourself. Even if you're speaking God's Word to others, be sure you don't do it in a combative style but rather in love, showing respect for others' opinions. World-renowned apologist Ravi Zaccharias has quoted an Indian proverb that went something like this: "Don't cut off a person's nose and then ask him to smell a rose."

So in any conversation, let's make an effort to hear the other person, and if we disagree, let's do so showing appropriate deference and reason. We just may learn something ourselves.

Prayer: God of all wisdom, help us to be open to what You are teaching us through Your Word and sometimes through the words of others. Keep us from being proud, and may we always be loving, kind, and respectful to others who have opinions that are different than ours, so that they may be drawn not just to us but to You working through us. In Jesus' name we pray. Amen.

P is for **Pure**

The LORD detests the thoughts of the wicked,
but those of the <u>pure</u> are pleasing to Him.
—Proverbs 15:26

Have you ever wondered how to please God? The answer to that question is in this proverb. He finds pleasure in the thoughts of the pure.

This is not the only place we read of this. In Psalm 24:3–5, we read,

> Who may ascend the hill of the LORD? Who may stand in His holy place? He who has clean hands and a pure heart, who does not lift up his soul unto an idol or swear by what is false. He will receive blessing from the LORD, and vindication from the God his Savior.

Another reference to this is in the beatitudes as taught in the Sermon on the Mount (Matthew 5:8) when Jesus says, "Blessed are the pure in heart, for they will see God."

God places a premium on pure thoughts because He is holy, and you'll notice that pureness is to be found in our thoughts. People can appear to be righteous, yet if we could read their minds or see their secret activities, we might find that their thoughts are far from pure.

Unfortunately, in this age and culture, purity of thought is more difficult than ever. We may be bombarded daily, even hourly, with sexual innuendoes, violence, and worse if we turn on the TV, go to the movies, or watch unfiltered Internet videos. Often at the office or places of learning, blasphemy and dirty stories abound. It's almost impossible to avoid hearing someone take the Lord's name in vain.

This has become so commonplace that many of us have become immune to it. Even if we don't act out or say unclean things ourselves, we are almost forced to have these thoughts enter our minds through our eyes and ears. As adults we <u>may</u> be able to refuse to dwell on these things, but think what these influences do to our children. Even many of the cartoons and G-rated movies that are produced have objectionable material subtly or blatantly introduced.

Are we guilty of evil thoughts which have become so "everyday" that we aren't even aware of our sin? The less time we spend with God, the more comfortable we will feel in the presence of those things or people that regularly spew out impure and unholy words and/or pictures.

Make a decision today to seek God's help in remaining pure in thought, for "as [a man] thinketh in his heart, so is he" (Proverbs 23:7 KJV).

Prayer: Most holy and compassionate Father, please protect our hearts and minds from the evil thoughts, words, and illustrations expressed so vividly around us. Forgive us for our tendency to allow these thoughts to penetrate into our being. Instead, Lord, fill us with Your Holy Spirit that there will be no room for ungodly thoughts and we may remain faithful in every area of our thought and life. In Jesus' name we pray. Amen.

(Do you evaluate your pureness by comparing your actions and thoughts to those of the people around you, or do you look for guidance from the Source of all purity as revealed in God's Word?)

Who can say, "I have kept my heart <u>pure</u>;
I am clean and without sin"?
—Proverbs 20:9

Even a child is known by his actions, by
whether his conduct is <u>pure</u> and right.
—Proverbs 20:11

He who loves a <u>pure</u> heart and whose speech is
gracious will have the king for his friend.
—Proverbs 22:11

There are those who curse their fathers and do not
bless their mothers; those who are <u>pure</u> in their
own eyes and yet are not cleansed of their filth.
—Proverbs 30:11, 12

 is for **Quarrelsome**

In the verses below, it seems quite apparent that being quarrelsome is most often a trait of women. Not that men don't have their bad qualities, but this seems to be especially prolific in women.

The unpleasantness of sharing a house with a quarrelsome wife is noted identically twice below in Proverbs 21:9 and 25:24. These were written by Solomon who had literally hundreds of wives and concubines, so surely he had much experience with quarrelsome wives. (He undoubtedly deserved all the miseries in that area he received for his uncontrolled desires.)

Women are notorious for their nagging, and it's such a useless exercise for it seldom does anything other than to make matters worse. We note in verse 26:21 below that when a man is quarrelsome, it's like he is igniting a fire—so the wife may not always be the instigator of unpleasantness.

Whatever our gender, we need to study ourselves to see what part we play in a home where there is discord. If our wife is nagging and complaining, does she have good reason to be? If our husband is ticked off, have we looked at the situation from his point of view and tried to talk reasonably rather than jump on him for whatever we perceive he is doing wrong?

Because we are of a different gender than our spouse, our thought processes are completely different also. Many times the things that get under our skin are off the radar of our mate and they just don't get it; therefore, our reactions seem unreasonable to them.

When you married, you adored one another and often gave up your desires while wanting to please each other. Now that you're married, keep the flame of love, which is sometimes easily blown out, protected by nourishing it with tender tinder. Do unexpected kindnesses (e.g., flowers for no special reason, a favorite meal prepared with candlelight and music in the background).

If you are preparing to marry (or even if you are already married), make a pact with each other that from now on when your feelings are hurt, instead of shouting or clamming up, you'll tell your mate you're upset and just can't talk about your problem then. Later when you're calmer, quietly explain your feelings (without accusations) so that your loved one can be more thoughtful in word or deed the next time—that goes for both husband and wife—and be sure if you're the offending party that you listen to what's being said. Sometimes this means going to a Christian counselor who can help you sort out your feelings and emotions. Even if it costs you, it's worth it.

One way to help ensure harmony and love within your marriage is to spend time together in prayer. Intentionally set time aside to read God's Word together (in addition to the time you spend alone with God). It's always good to read the Bible and pray together before you go to bed at night, for it's pretty hard to be angry with someone you're praying with and for.

At any rate, know that it's best to share a home where there is harmony and love, and this can be done as you seek God's blessing and work at making your spouse happy.

Prayer: Dear God of peace and harmony, insert Your nature into us so that we may with Your help be blessed in our relationship with our beloved one. Give us patience, wisdom, mercy, and kindness toward each other so that our marriage and friendships may blossom and grow more beautiful every day of our lives. In Jesus' name we ask this. Amen.

(A successful marriage is not often formed by a whirlwind courtship or a prelude of sexual intimacy. Take your time to get to know this person and their family in different settings. Contrariness usually manifests itself regularly if it is an issue in a person's life. Beware if it's bothersome early on, for this seldom changes after marriage and usually deteriorates what could have been a joyful life of sharing and intimacy.)

A foolish son is his father's ruin, and a
quarrelsome wife is like a constant dripping.
—Proverbs 19:13

Better to live on a corner of the roof than
share a house with a quarrelsome wife.
—Proverbs 21:9

Better to live in a desert than with a
quarrelsome and ill-tempered wife.
—Proverbs 21:19

Better to live on a corner of the roof than
share a house with a quarrelsome wife.
—Proverbs 25:24

As charcoal to embers and as wood to fire, so
is a quarrelsome man for kindling strife.
—Proverbs 26:21

A quarrelsome wife is like a constant dripping
on a rainy day; restraining her is like restraining
the wind or grasping oil with the hand.
—Proverbs 27:15, 16

is for **Right**

There is a way that seems <u>right</u> to a man,
but in the end it leads to death.
—Proverbs 14:12

There is a way that seems <u>right</u> to a man,
but in the end it leads to death.
—Proverbs 16:25

Here we have two identical verses, and there are other proverbs which speak of man's ideas on what is right such as Proverbs 12:15. "The way of a fool seems right to him, but a wise man listens to advice."

It seems that we can easily delude ourselves or be deluded into thinking wrong is right. Sometimes we do this because it seems everyone around us thinks it (whatever "it" is) is right so it must be right. Other times, we think something is right because we want it to be right; it makes us feel good or soothes our conscience to do so.

These days, many of us have come to the conclusion that there is no universal truth. What's right for you may not be right for me and vice versa; consequently, we do what we want to do.

"If it feels good, do it," we say, or "As long as what I do doesn't hurt anyone else, it's okay," convincing ourselves that our sin is a personal matter—though it may ultimately cause a broken home, children who know no boundaries, a chain of lies, or other harmful results not recognized as the initial sin is enacted. Indeed, in this day and age, the word *sin* is politically incorrect and most do not want to hear it.

When we have no anchor, we go whatever way the tide flows, which is why we need the Lord and His Word. If we do not recognize God as our Lord, then we feel free to act in whatever way we see fit, basically making ourselves a god. In doing this, we drift here and there with nothing to keep us secure. We can easily overlook or explain away a "little white lie," cheating on our taxes, having sex outside of marriage (since "everybody does it"), watching television shows with graphically immoral scenes because they're "funny," and playing or allowing our children to play violent and often immoral games on iPods or other Internet media where these perversions can be shared with friends.

So many things in today's culture have become okay which even fifty or sixty years ago were completely unacceptable—even to those who did not believe in God. But now our god has become entertainment and pleasure, which we will do most anything to obtain. We are bombarded daily in the media with messages that titillate our senses and encourage us to indulge in whatever we desire. No wonder the divorce rate is over the top for even Christians, and it should not be a surprise that our children are being killed by other children so that even the schools are not safe.

Our country, which generally used to be a haven for its citizens, is turning into a war zone. Yes, as our featured verses tell us, there is a way that seems right to a man, but in the end it leads to death. We, however, do not have to go the way of man. God has provided a different way when He sent His Son to die for us that we might through Him overcome our sin and have eternal life—not death and judgment. Jesus said, "I am the Way and the Truth and the Life. No one comes to the Father except through Me" (John 14:6).

Let us turn away from those things which would cause us to go astray and give our attention to God and His Word. This is the only way that we will be able to avoid eternal death. Instead we will find security in our God that will carry us through life's difficulties. Not that they will go away but that He will be with us to lead and guide us through these times and ultimately to our heavenly home, where there will be no more pain or suffering. In fact, our life will be full and exciting as we meet face-to-face our Lord, the Creator of all things, and the One who will provide wonderful events and activities which we cannot begin to imagine.

Prayer: Dear Father and Lord of heaven and earth, help us to seek to do what is right according to the teachings of Jesus Christ—not according to what seems right in the eyes of man—so that our end will not be death but eternal life. And Father, we know that we can't do this unless Your Holy Spirit indwells us, so please forgive our sins and come into our hearts so that we may live for You. We praise and thank You, dear Lord. Amen.

(We can't do what is right if we don't know what is right; we can't know what is right if we don't have wisdom; and we can't have wisdom unless we know the very Source of wisdom: Jesus Christ. As we come to know Him, we will want to read His Word and will gain a practical knowledge of right, including the insight given in the verses below.)

> [Proverbs are] for acquiring a disciplined and prudent
> life, doing what is <u>right</u> and just and fair.
> —Proverbs 1:3

> [My son, if you accept my words] Then you will understand
> what is <u>right</u> and just and fair—every good path.
> —Proverbs 2:9

> Listen for I [wisdom] have worthy things to say; I
> open my lips to speak what is <u>right</u>. My mouth speaks
> what is true, for my lips detest wickedness. All the

words of my mouth are just; none of them is crooked
or perverse. To the discerning all of them are <u>right</u>;
they are faultless to those who have knowledge.
—Proverbs 8:6–9

The way of a fool seems <u>right</u> to him,
but a wise man listens to advice.
—Proverbs 12:15

The first to present his case seems <u>right</u>, till
another comes forward and questions him.
—Proverbs 18:17

Even a child is known by his actions, by
whether his conduct is pure and <u>right</u>.
—Proverbs 20:11

All a man's ways seem <u>right</u> to him, but the
Lord weighs the heart. To do what is <u>right</u> and is
more acceptable to the Lord than sacrifice.
—Proverbs 21:2, 3

The violence of the wicked will drag them
away, for they refuse to do what is <u>right</u>.
—Proverbs 21:7

My son, if your heart is wise, then my heart
will be glad; my inmost being will rejoice
when your lips speak what is <u>right</u>.
—Proverbs 23:15, 16

Listen, my son, and be wise, and keep
your heart on the <u>right</u> path.
—Proverbs 23:19

 is for **Succeed**

A bribe is a charm to the one who gives
it; wherever he turns, he <u>succeeds</u>.
—Proverbs 17:8

There is no wisdom, no insight, no plan
that can <u>succeed</u> against the Lord.
—Proverbs 21:30

When we meditate on the above verses, they seem to be at odds with one another. In verse 17:8, are we being told we can get ahead by bribing those who can get us what we want? How does that tie in with the next verse, which indicates that we cannot succeed in anything if we make our plans outside of God's will?

As we study the Bible, we find that the God-inspired authors of the various books and letters *tell it like it is*. For instance, although David was "a man after [God's] own heart," (Acts 13:22) the author of 1 Samuel did not hide his human frailties and make him seem perfect. Even so, as we know from the writings throughout the Bible, God does not condone evil. Yet in spite of that, sometimes people who are evil do prosper in this world.

It appears, therefore, that the writer is simply acknowledging the fact that bribery can bring success in this world, at least for a time.

On the other hand, true success cannot be accomplished if we plot against the Lord and leave God out of our lives.

Sometimes we humans think that we can control our own destiny, that we are able to do whatever we set our mind to, that we don't need God.

God has certainly blessed us with whatever brains and intelligence we have, and He wants us to use them for His purposes. However, we forget that all that we have comes from Him—even our very being. Frequently it is not until we fail, find ourselves in life-threatening situations, or lose a loved one that we come back to reality. It is then that we come to understand that we have only so much control. It is God Who is the ultimate source of our wisdom and abilities.

There are those who refuse to acknowledge God and die in their sins. A case in point is Voltaire who lived during the 1700s. He was an avid atheist, very forthright in his belief that there is no God, and he mocked Him at every opportunity. He made a statement indicating that in a few more years, no one would believe in God, that He would completely be out of the picture. Voltaire died. Years later, the Geneva Bible Society purchased his home, the very residence where that man had lived in Geneva, Switzerland, and God's Word was sent all over the world from there.[4]

The Lord does not have to prove Himself to us, though proof of Him is easily seen in all His creation if we are willing to see it. Many have tried to test God by saying, "If there is a God, let Him do …" And when He doesn't respond, they think that proves that He doesn't exist. How foolish. God is not accountable to us, but we are accountable to Him. If we choose to resist Him and close our eyes to the evidences of His existence, then we have chosen to spend eternity away from Him in a place called hell. God does not send us there; we send ourselves. For He loved us so much that no one has to go there unless they choose to do so. He gave His Son to die and rise again so that if we accept Him into our hearts and repent of our sins, our salvation is guaranteed.

From Adam and Eve at the beginning of time until today, man has rebelled against God. His Word has been prohibited from societies and civilizations, seemingly completely demolished from a country, only to sprout up in another generation in that same country with more vibrancy and life. Even as a nation or cult persecutes its Christians and tries to purge the land of all faith in God, new converts seem to be set on fire by the Holy Spirit in the most unlikely places. (Witness the amazing growth of Christianity among the Middle East countries where ISIS is terrorizing and butchering innocent people.)

Let us acknowledge the truth of the scripture noted above— "There is no wisdom, no insight, no plan that can succeed against the LORD"—and bow our knees and our hearts to the God of the universe.

Prayer: God of love, hear my prayer to You as I remember the sacrifice Your Son made for me by dying on the cross. Give me the desire and the will to repent and put my life in Your hands so that I may find true success—knowing the joy of Your favor and the promise of eternal life. I ask this in Jesus' name. Amen.

(Following the advice of these additional verses below will assist you in finding success in ways that are pleasing to the Lord.)

> Plans fail for lack of counsel, but with
> many advisers they <u>succeed</u>.
> —Proverbs 15:22

> Commit to the LORD whatever you do,
> and your plans will <u>succeed</u>.
> —Proverbs 16:3

 is for **Trust**

Whoever gives heed to instruction prospers,
and blessed is he who <u>trusts</u> in the LORD.
—Proverbs 16:20

In this verse, we see that those who trust in the Lord will be blessed as they obey Him.

There are times when we will receive instructions contrary to God's will. The Lord surely does not want us to follow that advice. If we truly trust in the Lord, we will do so because we know Him, and we will only get to know Him and His will for our lives as we study His Word. The more we get to know Him, the more pleasure we will have in spending time with Him. It will become our heart's desire to draw closer to Him.

Do you find reading the Bible a bore? Are you so "busy" that you can't take even five minutes each day looking for His wisdom, reading the words He has prepared for us?

When you receive a letter, a text, or an e-mail from a dear friend, think how eagerly you read it. Depending on how warm your feelings for this friend are, you may read it over and over again.

If we truly love the Lord with all our heart, then we will be anxious to learn of His love for us. In times of distress, we will know where to turn for comfort. We will know that while those around us may disappoint, even at times betray us, our heavenly Father is ever present and ready to encourage and cheer us. The closer we draw to Him, the more we will trust Him.

Life will present us with many heartaches and sorrows, but as we mature in our knowledge of Him, His grace, mercy, and kindness will become more and more apparent to us. His presence will be so real that we will be able to deal with whatever problems face us.

How wonderful to know the Lord not only as our Savior but also as our dearest friend. Take advantage of the blessings He has in store for you by trusting Him wholeheartedly each day.

Prayer: Heavenly Father, thank You for Your love to us even when we fail to trust in You. Help us to seek Your wisdom so that we may heed Your instructions. Open the gates of blessings waiting for us, which we have inhibited by neglecting to take the time to learn more of You. All glory belongs to You, dear Father, Son, and Holy Spirit. Amen.

(It's important to know whom and what to trust. To gain such knowledge, we need to heed His Word and seek His wisdom.)

> <u>Trust</u> in the LORD with all your heart and lean not on
> your own understanding; in all your ways acknowledge
> Him and He will make your paths straight.
> —Proverbs 3:5, 6

> Whoever <u>trusts</u> in his riches will fall, but the
> righteous will thrive like a green leaf.
> —Proverbs 11:28

> A wise man attacks the city of the mighty and
> pulls down the stronghold in which they <u>trust</u>.
> —Proverbs 21:22

So that your <u>trust</u> may be in the L<small>ORD</small>,
I teach you today, even you.
—Proverbs 22:19

Wounds from a friend can be <u>trusted</u>
but an enemy multiplies kisses.
—Proverbs 27:6

A greedy man stirs up dissension, but he
who <u>trusts</u> in the L<small>ORD</small> will prosper.
—Proverbs 28:25

He who <u>trusts</u> in himself is a fool, but he
who walks in wisdom is kept safe.
—Proverbs 28:26

Fear of man will prove to be a snare, but
whoever <u>trusts</u> in the L<small>ORD</small> is kept safe.
—Proverbs 29:25

is for **Unpunished**

Be sure of this: The wicked will not go <u>unpunished</u>,
but those who are righteous will go free.
—Proverbs 11:21

Is this really true? Are the wicked punished? Are the righteous free from punishment?

We may at times question the sentiments of this verse, for in our life experiences this does not always appear to be the case. We are disillusioned with our justice system when it seems that crimes have been committed but punishment has not been meted out or has been meted out improperly. In fact, in these days when there seems to be a war on God and people of faith, and when efforts are being made to dismantle the US Constitution and replace it with international laws, we see the courts skewing justice—at times punishing the innocent and releasing the guilty.

Our children are being indoctrinated with the idea that truth is relative. Their morals are built on shifting sands, and they are flailing around, insecure, with nothing in which to anchor their lives. As a result, we are seeing violence escalating, honesty and integrity becoming nonexistent, morality defined by each person as to what they want it to be, and righteousness often treated as a joke.

Through it all, even as man declares himself to be the ultimate authority, God reigns. He has allowed Satan to woo and tempt mankind to sin, and He has permitted man to make the choice for good or evil. However, His Word is close to being translated into every language, and this goal may very well be accomplished in another decade. He is making provision for all nations and peoples of the earth to learn of His love for them. While His people may be mentally harassed and physically abused, even killed—in their martyrdom, many others are being drawn to the God these martyrs worshipped so faithfully.

Though in one area of the earth, zeal and love for God appear to be fading, in other most unlikely locations Christianity is exploding, in spite of (and perhaps because of) persecution by ungodly, evil forces.

So how does this reconcile with the key verse and the verses below? It seems that the godly are being punished and the ungodly have control.

Looking at life from man's viewpoint, this often seems to be the case; however, if we could get a God's-eye view and eternal perspective, we would see that our lives on this earth are miniscule in eternity. Whatever suffering we do for Christ's sake here on earth is nothing compared to the eternity of glory and joy we will experience after death.

Conversely, those who choose to reject God's gift of salvation through Jesus Christ and deliberately choose unrighteousness will enter eternal punishment when their time on this earth comes to an end.

If you think you're good and don't need to humble yourself before God, accepting Christ as your Savior, notice Proverbs 16:5 below. The Lord detests prideful hearts, and your eternity will be spent in torment just as an unrepentant murderer's or any other sinner who has not sought God's forgiveness and grace. How can this be? Because by rejecting God's Son, you have been guilty of crucifying Him, as if you had been there when He was nailed on the cross and chose not to get involved.

So please, please, for God's sake, turn to Him now. He loves you; He's waiting with open arms to receive you into His kingdom. May the words of this beautiful hymn below be our prayer in seeking reconciliation with the God who loves us more than life itself.

> Just as I am, without one plea, But that Thy blood was shed for me,
>
> And that Thou bidd'st me come to Thee, O Lamb of God, I come! I come!
>
> Just as I am, and waiting not To rid my soul of one dark blot,
>
> To Thee Whose blood can cleanse each spot, O Lamb of God, I come! I come!
>
> Just as I am, tho' tossed about With many a conflict, many a doubt,
>
> Fightings and fears within without, O Lamb of God, I come! I come!
>
> Just as I am, Thou wilt receive, Wilt welcome, pardon, cleanse, relieve;
>
> Because Thy promise I believe, O Lamb of God, I come! I come!
>
> Just as I am, Thy love unknown Hath broken ev'ry barrier down;
>
> Now to be Thine, yea, Thine alone, O Lamb of God, I come! I come![5]

(God makes plain to us those things that we do that result in punishment and His wrath.)

Can a man scoop fire into his lap without his clothes being burned? Can a man walk on hot coals without his feet being scorched? So is he who sleeps with another man's wife; no one who touches her will go <u>unpunished</u>.
—Proverbs 6:27–29

The LORD detests all the proud of heart. Be sure of this: They will not go <u>unpunished</u>.
—Proverbs 16:5

He who mocks the poor shows contempt for their Maker; whoever gloats over disaster will not go <u>unpunished</u>.
—Proverbs 17:5

A false witness will not go <u>unpunished</u>, and he who pours out lies will not go free.
—Proverbs 19:5

A false witness will not go <u>unpunished</u>, and he who pours out lies will perish.
—Proverbs 19:9

A faithful man will be richly blessed, but one eager to get rich will not go <u>unpunished</u>.
—Proverbs 28:20

 is for **Vent**

A fool gives full <u>vent</u> to his anger, but a wise
man keeps himself under control.
—Proverbs 29:11

It's so embarrassing to find yourself in a restaurant with friends and, when the meal is served, one member of your party explodes in anger because something about the food is not right. With a loud voice and hateful words, he lashes out at the waitress, bringing shame on himself and those at the table and causing the waitress humiliation and distress.

No matter who does this, it's wrong, but if it's someone who purports to be a Christian, what a terrible impression he leaves about his faith on those around him. When we take the name *Christian*, it indicates (or should indicate) that we are no longer the master of our heart and mind—that we have given our lives over to the One we call Savior and do those things that reflect His goodness and love. When we fail to do this, we have sinned against God, our fellow Christians, and those who have been affected by whatever sinful deed we have done.

Of course, none of us is perfect, and even as Christians we will find ourselves displaying behavior that grieves our Lord. If we truly love Him, however, these actions should diminish as we draw nearer to Him each day. We should always feel remorse and seek forgiveness when they occur—not only from God but also from the ones we have wronged. If this is not the case, then we should question the sincerity of our commitment and whether we have truly in our hearts asked Christ to be our Savior and Lord. For once we have asked Him into our being, we should never again be able to be happy and comfortable when we have allowed sinful thoughts, words, or deeds to displace the fruit of the Spirit: love, joy, peace, patience, kindness goodness, faithfulness, gentleness, and self-control. (See Galatians 5:22, 23 KJV.)

Prayer: Our loving heavenly Father, give us wisdom and strength to do Your will and walk in Your way. Please keep us from flying off the handle when things don't go our way and from any other sinful ways so that our lives may be channels through which You may display Your loving kindness. We pray in the name of Your Precious Son, our Savior and Lord. Amen.

 is for **Wait**

Do not say, "I'll pay you back for this wrong!"
<u>Wait</u> for the LORD, and he will deliver you.
—Proverbs 20:22

Wait. Who likes to wait? We're on our way home and want to pick up just an item or two from the grocery store for supper. It should only take a minute, right? Wrong! We get behind someone in line at the checkout who has a problem and instead of a minute, it's fifteen or twenty before we get on our way.

Or maybe we're on our way to work. Uh-oh. We're caught behind a school bus and there's no way to get past. It stops every few minutes. The ride to work which should have taken ten minutes takes at least twice that long.

Those things are annoying but in the long run are just little bumps along the way. The really hard things are another story. For instance, when you marry someone that you dearly love and who promises to love and cherish you but in a few years you discover that that person has cheated on you, love turns to bitterness and anger. How easy it is to retaliate. We read a verse like the above and think, *Yeah, sure, get real.*

The idea of waiting on the Lord when we are wronged, especially when it hurts so much, seems ridiculous. Our natural reaction is to get even, to try to hurt them as badly as they have hurt us. How in the world are we supposed to wait on the Lord? We want to take action, and we want to do it *NOW*.

It's times like that that our faith is really tested. It's hard for us to believe that "in all things God works for the good of those who love Him, who have been called according to his purpose" (Romans 8:28). How can anything good come out of this? *He (or she) needs to be taught a lesson,* we think. Our mind is filled with ideas of how we can hurt the other person. We dream of how good we'll feel to see them miserable.

Yet that's not God's way. If we insist on hurting our adversary, it seldom satisfies. It's never enough, and often the other person finds ways to bring more pain into our life. And so the "war" escalates and takes on a life of its own, with hatred controlling our thoughts and actions. If there are children involved, their pain is intensified as they see their mom and dad in this battle of retribution.

So how can we deal with such a situation? Perhaps that's why God tells us to wait on Him. For one thing, if we wait instead of responding immediately in anger, our emotions are not so high and we can see more clearly. When we've given ourselves time to stop and think about the situation, though the hurt is still there, we may be able to talk through the pain and suffering the other person has caused. We may discover reasons why this happened, which didn't make it right but gives us an understanding of the other person's stress and shame—if indeed they are ashamed. We will also have time to think of the times we have betrayed God's love for us and realize how forgiving God has been to us. When that happens, it helps us to start on our journey of forgiveness toward the one who betrayed us.

Some such problems actually have a happy ending where the marriage or friendship is saved and even enhanced as the understanding of one another grows and with it the love or concern for each other. However, we all know that that is often not the case. Yet as we wait on the Lord, even if the other person continues on their selfish path and does not seek forgiveness but instead refuses to make peace and goes their own way, God works within our hearts and gives us a strength we never knew we had. Sometimes God uses us to help others who are having a similar experience. Sometimes it draws us even closer to Him, for we recognize that without Him, we are hopeless. Often if we are faithful in waiting on Him, our life turns out to be much better than we had ever imagined even though it may be eons apart from what we had hoped for originally.

There are many ways other people can hurt us, but the choice is always ours as to how we react. If we trust in the Lord, we can know that whatever the pain we suffer, He is with us through it all and He will make things right—if not in this world then in the next. Even if, in the world's eyes, life is unfair, our relationship with Him will become so precious that it will sustain us through all our days on earth—something that would most likely not have happened if we hadn't had to suffer through this ordeal.

Prayer: Loving, faithful Father, thank You so much that You never let us down. As we face the disappointments and failures in our lives, may we learn to wait on You that we may find the blessings You are so eager to share with us. In Jesus' precious name we pray. Amen.

(Waiting doesn't always mean doing nothing. We need to be active in our watching and praying for the good Lord's help to get us through the situation.)

Blessed is the man who listens to me [wisdom],
watching daily at my doors, <u>waiting</u> at my doorway.
—Proverbs 8:34

 is for **eXalt**

Righteousness <u>exalts</u> a nation, but sin
is a disgrace to any people.
—Proverbs 14:34

There was a time when people longed to be thought of as righteous, honest, and honorable, and thankfully there are still some who desire this. However, as we hear, watch, and read the news, it seems that these virtues are not priorities for the mass of people. Sin is blatantly trumpeted and encouraged in our society. Shame is almost unknown. When was the last time you saw anyone blush?

To extol righteousness these days is to swim against the tide. In our beloved country (the United States), some of our presidents have not only acted immorally but lied about it, and when caught in their lies, they continued on as if it was of little consequence. No wonder our children are cynical and often develop into characterless people.

And let's not allow all the blame to fall on the backs of well-known, influential people. The positions they have achieved have often been because of us. We do the voting (or nonvoting, should we shirk our responsibility), pay for the movie tickets or the DVDs that condone—even promote—those kind of actions, and sadly often participate ourselves in immorality (lying, gossip, sex outside of marriage, etc.).

A nation is only as good as the people who live in it. If we, as people, live lives that are sinful and/or refuse to take a stand on what is right, then we can expect the whole country to be rotten to the core.

The only way for us to reverse the situation is to truly love the Lord with all our hearts and to love our neighbors as ourselves. God has given us His Word so that we may know of His love for us and so we may learn how to show our love for Him.

Because our world has been taken over by sin and our ideas have been shaped by the influence of an ungodly world, we may not understand how to love. We often think that love is a feeling. Therefore, if a feeling changes, that means that love is gone. God's Word teaches us that while feeling may well be a part of love, it is minimal compared to the whole concept. As we read in 1 Corinthians 13:4–7,

> Love is patient, love is kind. It does not envy, it does not boast, it is not proud. It is not rude, it is not self-seeking, it is not easily angered, it keeps no record of wrongs. Love does not delight in evil but rejoices with the truth. It always protects, always trusts, always hopes, always perseveres.

Can you imagine what kind of country our nation would be if we returned to the faith of our fathers who espoused these truths? What if we became a nation whose people looked for ways to help and nurture one another instead of trying to get ahead at any cost? A nation where the leaders of our land could be trusted to tell the truth and value life? A nation whose entertainment industry produced DVDs, films, magazines, Internet content, etc. that celebrated faithfulness, kindness, obedience, and truth? A nation whose people lived as Jesus taught and supported those leaders and industries that not only produced good products but were bastions of integrity also.

Wow! Gone would be phony news stories that only project politically correct views. Gone would be the promotion of twisted truth in educational institutions where students are degraded for their faith in God—sometimes even failed for their faith though having had proven excellence in their studies. Gone would be the marketing of known faulty equipment in order to make an extra buck. Gone would be the industry of lawyers whose only cases were built on suing industries with "deep pockets" for ridiculous claims such as people getting burned because they held their coffee between their knees while driving. Gone would be the covering up of doctors with faulty medical practices by medical associations while at the same time having a plan for discipline which could be administered making the suing of doctors, who in good faith did their best to provide good medical care, invalid.

Righteousness by the people makes righteousness of a nation possible.

While no nation or its people can ever be perfect, if the goal of the nation is to be so, then the killing of babies in the womb, the selling of drugs, the violence in schools and homes, drunk driving, immorality, and so many other crimes would become minimal and this country would be exalted and gain the respect in which it was once held by all the nations of the world.

Prayer: Oh God of justice, goodness, and righteousness, give us hearts that long for Your Spirit to indwell us so that we may exemplify in our daily lives the virtues that make a country exalted. We know this can only be done through our willingness and desire to have Jesus Christ as our Savior and Lord. Enter our hearts today that we may start on our journey to lives of righteousness. Thank You, Lord. Amen.

(To be truly exalted, the exalting must be
done by others, not by ourselves.)

Esteem [wisdom], and she will <u>exalt</u> you;
embrace her, and she will honor you.
—Proverbs 4:8

Through the blessing of the upright a city is <u>exalted</u>,
but by the mouth of the wicked it is destroyed.
—Proverbs 11:11

Do not <u>exalt</u> yourself in the king's presence, and
do not claim a place among great men; it is better
for him to say to you, "Come up here," than for
him to humiliate you before a nobleman.
—Proverbs 25:6, 7a

If you have played the fool and <u>exalted</u> yourself, or if you
have planned evil, clap your hand over your mouth! For
as churning the milk produces butter, and as twisting the
nose produces blood, so stirring up anger produces strife.
—Proverbs 30:32, 33

is for **Yet**

A man's own folly ruins his life, <u>yet</u> his
heart rages against the LORD.
—Proverbs 19:3

This key verse is so true. How often we see people do stupid, sometimes evil and wicked things, and then blame God when their lives are a mess? There are those who immediately fault God when anything goes wrong, whether it's personal such as a car accident or a natural disaster such as a flood. How inconsistent they are. These same people never give God praise for an accident averted (that was "luck") or for the miraculous recovery from an illness against all odds (once again, it was "luck").

In Jesus' ministry as He told His parables, He often ended with the phrase "He who has ears to hear, let him hear." It may have been Dr. David Jeremiah who said this was like our present day comment, "If the shoe fits, wear it." These parables, which were allegorical, gave messages in picturesque language to educate and sometimes convict those who heard. While some were not always clear to the listeners, there were others that the hearers could clearly understand but did not want to acknowledge pertained to them, such as the parable of the Prodigal Son with the unforgiving older brother representing the Pharisees.

The Pharisees closed their ears to Jesus' teachings and came to hate Him enough to have Him killed. They postured themselves as holy and righteous, performing rituals publicly and having much fanfare when they gave to the temple treasury so that everyone would be impressed with their goodness. Of course, all the while they were actually raging against the Lord Jesus, as their foolish desires led them into jealousy and evil plans against the Son of the very God they were supposed to be worshipping.

Although a few of these Pharisees and other leaders did come to know Christ as their Savior, sadly most of them, it seems, destroyed themselves spiritually because of their foolish hardheadedness toward our Lord.

Before we condemn them too strongly, however, let us step back and survey our own thoughts and actions in relation to Jesus Christ. Have we, too, been caught up in such hypocrisy? Have we done good things publicly so that others would be impressed with our goodness yet privately nursed thoughts and desires, even practiced deeds that would be displeasing to our Lord?

Prayer: Dear Father, help us to not be concerned with condemning others for their sinful ways but to seek Your wisdom in remaining true to You ourselves, doing those things that will be in line with Your will for our lives. Blessed be Your Son, our Savior Jesus Christ, in Whose name we pray. Amen.

(It's interesting to see how the little word *yet* connects a thought that tends to lead our thinking in one direction yet often draws us to a different conclusion with another thought. Notice how the author uses this little word in the following verses.)

Go to the ant, you sluggard; consider its ways and be wise!
It has no commander, no overseer or ruler, <u>yet</u> it stores its
provisions in summer and gathers its food at harvest.
—Proverbs 6:6–8

One man gives freely, <u>yet</u> gains even more; another
withholds unduly; but comes to poverty.
—Proverbs 11:24

One man pretends to be rich, <u>yet</u> has nothing;
another pretends to be poor <u>yet</u> has great wealth.
—Proverbs 13:7

To show partiality is not good—<u>yet</u> a man
will do wrong for a piece of bread.
—Proverbs 28:21

There are those who curse their fathers and do not
bless their mothers; those who are pure in their
own eyes and <u>yet</u> are not cleansed of their filth.
—Proverbs 30:11–12

Four things on earth are small, <u>yet</u> they are extremely wise:
Ants are creatures of little strength, <u>yet</u> they store up their
food in the summer; coneys are creatures of little power,
<u>yet</u> they make their home in the crags; locusts have no
king, <u>yet</u> they advance together in ranks; a lizard can be
caught with the hand, <u>yet</u> it is found in kings' palaces.
—Proverbs 30:24–28

Z is for **Zeal**

It is not good to have <u>zeal</u> without knowledge,
nor to be hasty and miss the way.
—Proverbs 19:2

Enthusiasm is a wonderful thing. Seeing a need and doing your best to take care of it as soon as possible is commendable. Surely the Lord will bless such actions. However, most of us know or have known someone who gets all hyped up over something without thinking it through. They hear something and, without getting the whole story, leap into action—often making matters worse instead of helping out.

We have a tendency to jump to conclusions and then say or do things which are at the least unhelpful and at the most downright painful to ourselves or others.

In this verse, we are warned not to rush into things, to know what we are doing before we take action or we may miss the way. This is where humbling ourselves and having an attitude of prayer instead of thinking we know it all will allow God to prompt us to do the right thing. This may mean immediate action, or it may mean to wait and study the situation more carefully until it becomes very clear what the course of action should be. As this becomes a way of life, we will find that we become wiser in our actions which will not only bring blessings on us but also on those around us. How satisfying it is when we find ourselves in the center of His will!

Prayer: Omniscient God, thank You that You know every detail of every life and situation. Help us to allow You to be in control of our lives, so that we do not lose our way in our enthusiasm to take action in matters in which we are not fully informed. May the things we do always reflect Your love toward others and a desire to do Your will.

(Our zeal should always be motivated by love for the Lord.)

Do not let your heart envy sinners, but always be
<u>zealous</u> for the fear of the LORD. There is surely a future
hope for you, and your hope will not be cut off.
—Proverbs 23:17, 18

Index of Biblical References

Endnotes

1   R. Laird Harris, Th.M, Ph.D., Professor of Old Testament, Covenant College and Theological Seminary, St. Louis, Mo., contributor to "The Book of Proverbs" in *The Wycliffe Bible Commentary*, copyright 1962 by The Moody Bible Institute of Chicago. Laird references the writings of two gentlemen: (1) Charles T.Fritsch. "The Book of Proverbs, Introduction and Exegesis," *Interpreter's Bible*. Vol. IV. New York and Nashville: Abingdon, 1955, and (2) W. O. E. Oesterley, *The Book of Proverbs*. New York: Dutton, 1929. and *The Wisdom of Egypt and the Old Testament*. London: Society for the Promotion of Christian Knowledge, 1927. These men indicate that the "sayings of the wise" are similar to writings from Egyptian literature.

2   Joseph Scriven. *What a Friend We Have in Jesus*. See PDHymns.com. Last update March 26, 2016. A collection of public domain hymns.

3   John Philip Sousa III. *Ben Carson, Rx for America*, 84 and 85.

4   Gleaned from information through Google in March 2015. Copyright © 1977 Theological Seminary. Ministers-best-friend.com/VOLTAIRE-His-Home-Used-As-BIBLE-SOCIETY—TRUTH-or-MYTH.html.

5   Charlotte Elliot. *Just as I Am*. See PDHymns.com. Last update March 26, 2016. A collection of public domain hymns.